GOD'S INCARNATE WORD

Study by Steve Sumerel
Commentary by Guy Sayles

Free downloadable Teaching Guide for this study available at
NextSunday.com/teachingguides

NextSunday Resources
6316 Peake Road
Macon, Georgia 31210-3960
1-800-747-3016

TABLE OF CONTENTS

God's Incarnate Word

HOW TO USE THIS STUDY

NextSunday Resources Adult Bible Studies are designed to help adults study Scripture seriously within the context of the larger Christian tradition and, through that process, find their faith renewed, challenged, and strengthened. We study the Scriptures because we believe they affect our current lives in important ways. Each study contains the following three components:

Study Guide

Each study guide lesson is arranged in four movements:

Reflecting recalls a contemporary story, anecdote, example, or illustration to help us anticipate the session's relevance in our lives.

Studying is centered on giving the biblical material in-depth attention while often surrounding it with helpful insights from theology, ethics, church history, and other areas.

Understanding helps us find relevant connections between our lives and the biblical message.

What About Me? provides brief statements that help unite life issues with the meaning of the biblical text.

Commentary

Each study guide lesson is accompanied by an additional, in-depth commentary on the biblical material. Written by a different author than the study guide, each commentary gives the opportunity for learners to approach the Scripture text from a separate but complementary viewpoint.

Teaching Guide

In addition to the provided study guide and commentary, *NextSunday Resources* also provides a *free* downloadable teaching guide, available at NextSunday.com. Each teaching guide gives the teacher tools for focusing on the content of each study guide lesson through additional commentary and Bible background information. Through teacher helps and teaching options, each teaching guide also provides substance for variety and choice in the preparation of each lesson.

NextSunday
Resources

STUDY INTRODUCTION

The Season of Advent is upon us, and we turn to the Gospel of John to move us toward the grand celebration of our Savior's birth. You might wonder why a Gospel that does not contain a nativity story would be chosen to take us through the Christmas season. The answer to this question is quite simple. Although John's Gospel does not say much about *how* Christ came to earth, it pays very close attention to *why* Christ came to be among us in the flesh.

Each lesson will delve into a portion of the tightly packed and beautifully expressed prologue, which comprises the first eighteen verses of the Gospel. These passages will be connected to an event in the ministry of Jesus that gives further insight into the meaning of the prologue.

John the Baptist is a major figure in this study as well. Although the writer of this Gospel does not develop the backstory of this extraordinary character in the way the other Gospels do, the power of the Baptist's message and the depth of meaning it contains are given in dynamic and dramatic style.

This unit will take us a bit off the beaten path of Advent studies. With no angels to sing for us and no shepherds to guide us to the manger, we are left to find a different pathway to the overwhelming reality of God's incarnation, the Word become flesh. In this study, the wise men do not lead us to the Christ child. Rather, the one who cries in the wilderness takes us to the water's edge and introduces us to the Lamb of God. We will not be invited to hear the cries of a baby at life's beginning, but to be present with God in the beginning of it all. This study will not ponder a star that hangs over the city of David, but will invite us to experience the reality of a light that shines untouched by darkness.

Welcome to Advent and to John's beautiful and bold account of God's incarnation.

THE LIGHT
SHINES IN THE DARKNESS
John 1:1-5; 9:1-7, 35-41

Central Question

What light has Jesus shined in my darkness?

Scripture

John 1:1-5

1 In the beginning was the Word and the Word was with God and the Word was God. 2 The Word was with God in the beginning. 3 Everything came into being through the Word, and without the Word nothing came into being. What came into being 4 through the Word was life, and the life was the light for all people. 5 The light shines in the darkness, and the darkness doesn't extinguish the light.

John 9:1-7, 35-41

1 As Jesus walked along, he saw a man who was blind from birth. 2 Jesus' disciples asked, "Rabbi, who sinned so that he was born blind, this man or his parents?" 3 Jesus answered, "Neither he nor his parents. This happened so that God's mighty works might be displayed in him. 4 While it's daytime, we must do the works of him who sent me. Night is coming when no one can work. 5 While I am in the world, I am the light of the world." 6 After he said this, he spit on the ground, made mud with the saliva, and smeared the mud on the man's eyes. 7 Jesus said to him, "Go, wash in the pool of Siloam" (this word means sent). So the man went away and washed. When he returned, he could see.... 35 Jesus heard they had expelled the man born blind. Finding him, Jesus said, "Do you believe in the Human One?"

36 He answered, "Who is he, sir? I want to believe in him." 37 Jesus said, "You have seen him. In fact, he is the one speaking with you." 38 The man said, "Lord, I believe." And he worshipped Jesus. 39 Jesus said, "I have come into the world to exercise judgment so that those who don't see can see and those who see will become blind." 40 Some Pharisees who were with him heard what he said and asked, "Surely we aren't blind, are we?" 41 Jesus said to them, "If you were blind, you wouldn't have any sin, but now that you say, 'We see,' your sin remains."

Reflecting

One of many wonderful stories Gene Rooney collected in his book *Amphorae* is called "The Closing Darkness." It is a story about an old man who comes to believe that he is losing his sight. His reaction to this belief is to put on dark glasses and close himself off in a darkened apartment. The darkness he creates in the room reinforces his belief that he will soon no longer be able to see.

When a new neighbor comes to visit, she insists on turning on lights, opening the curtains, and cleaning the dingy windows. The old man curses this young lady and her efforts. After spending so much time in the darkness, the light is painful to him. He even accuses the young lady of trying to hurt him. The story leaves the reader realizing that it can be easier to live in darkness than to bear the pain of being exposed to the light.

The season of Advent has begun. It is good that we celebrate the season with bright lights adorning trees, houses, and city streets. Let the lights of the season remind us that we celebrate the coming of the one who brought a wonderful light into a very dark world. It was a light that many tried to shut out, and it is a light that the world has tried to extinguish. But we celebrate a light that outshines all the darkness of the world and all of the efforts to put it out.

As we enter the Christmas season, open your curtains and take off your dark glasses. Dare to see the light.

Studying

The Word and the Light. We do not know who wrote the Fourth Gospel, but early tradition identifies John, son of Zebedee, as "the [disciple] whom Jesus loved" (John 13:23; 20:2; see 21:20-24). This disciple, whoever he was, is identified as the authority behind the stories of Jesus contained in this Gospel.

The Gospel begins with a prologue (John 1:1-18). This well-crafted poem or hymn makes clear who Jesus is. The language of the prologue speaks clearly to believers in Jesus, both Jews and Gentiles. John connects Jesus to the story of God's creation of the world as found in Genesis 1 by starting with the words "In the beginning" (see Gen 1:1, NRSV).

A key term in the author's prologue is "Word" (Greek, *logos*). Readers might have heard this term in a number of ways. For Jews, God's "Word" was an aspect or manifestation of God's self. God created the universe, after all, by speaking it into existence. Jews would understand the Word of God as God's energy to bring life and order out of chaos. Drawing on Hebrew wisdom traditions, especially Proverbs 8–9, many Jews also equated "the Word of God" with God's wisdom—the governing principle by which God created the world.

At the same time, Greek philosophy also had much to say about "the Word." In some philosophical schools, *logos* signified the ordering principle of the universe. It was this principle that brought the world into being and holds it together.

The earliest Christians brought this multifaceted understanding of *logos* into their theology in order to speak of the redemptive ministry of God. Following in the tradition of the Old Testament prophets, the "word of God" was the message the apostles proclaimed to the world.

Which of these aspects of "the Word" might John have intended? It is likely he wanted his readers to perceive something of them all. In his commentary on John, William Hull suggests that the Word could be viewed as either a divine power, a rational principle, or a redemptive proclamation (212). Clearly, John was making the point that Jesus embodies all of these things.

John carefully connects the dots: the Word was life, and that life is the light. John leaves no doubt that Jesus embodies all the rich connotations of the Word, and that his light cannot be extinguished even by all the darkness evident in the world. The rest of John's Gospel shows Jesus bringing the light of God's power, truth, and redemptive nature to all who will dare see it.

Redefining Blindness. When the disciples encounter the man who has been blind from birth, they wonder about the cause of such a severe condition. It was commonly held in ancient times that blindness and other physical afflictions resulted from punishment of sin. It is quite understandable that the disciples would have accepted such notions.

Because this man was blind from birth, some might have speculated that he was being punished for something his parents did. Some, however, wondered about the possibility of sinning even in the womb. The story of Jacob grasping his brother Esau's heel (Gen 25:24-25) gave at least a kernel of validity to this theory in the eyes of some (see O'Day, 653).

The disciples asked Jesus to weigh in on the issue. He responds by addressing not the blindness of the man but the blindness of his own disciples. You might say that Jesus first initiated a miracle of sight by helping the disciples to see clearly. By redirecting their unproductive discussion, Jesus helped them see the real meaning of this blind man's story.

Jesus then made mud from his saliva and put it on the man's eyes. Then he had the man wash in the ceremonial waters of Siloam. As soon as he did so, the man who was blind could suddenly see. The result was tremendous for the man, but even more so for all those who witnessed it. This miracle gave them something new to consider as they pondered the nature of God.

The Pool of Siloam, sometimes referred to as the "Old Pool," was fed by an open canal from the pool of Gihon. It was commonly used by sick people to wash in the belief that it had healing powers. It was also the source of water used in the final day of the Feast of Tabernacles, which will be of importance in session 3.

Unfortunately, Jesus' miracle provoked resistance. Learning of the event, Jesus' opponents tried to fit him into their preconceived boxes, even if doing so meant threatening the recipient of the healing. The Pharisees absolutely refused to see the reality in front of their eyes.

The ending of this narrative comes in two parts. First, Jesus finds the man who had been blind. Next, he confronts the Jewish authorities. Read together, these episodes reveal what sight and blindness really mean.

The final encounter between the man who was blind and Jesus comes when Jesus seeks him out. Confronted with the reality of who Jesus is, the newly sighted man's confession of faith reveals that he was the recipient of both physical sight and, more importantly, of spiritual sight. His new eyes help him see new truth revealed in Jesus.

The story ends, however, with an encounter between Jesus and the Jewish elite. Their arrogance is revealed in their question, "Surely we aren't blind, are we?" (John 9:40). The irony of this question should not be lost on us. They claimed clarity of sight while failing to recognize the one to whom they were talking. Jesus reveals that God is patient with those who know they can't see, but stands in judgment on those who are blind to their own blindness.

Why do we resist gaining knowledge that might cause us to change our opinions?

Understanding

The Gospel of John (and the whole Bible, for that matter) builds a case that God's truth, revealed through Christ, is accessible to everyone. But not everyone receives it. The light of revelation shines brightly, but we must open our eyes to see it.

The story of the blind man reveals that ironic truth. Like the Jerusalem authorities, the more we *think* we can see, the less likely we are able to recognize our own blindness. At the same time, the one who is blind and knows it is richly blessed with both physical and spiritual sight.

John 9 reveals two ways we turn away from what God wants us to see. First, like the disciples, we look for answers to the wrong questions. The disciples were pondering whose sin was responsible for the man's blindness. Such an argument might occupy them for hours, but would inevitably take them only to the end of a dead-end street. Good magicians make their illusions work by drawing our attention away from the point where the trick would be revealed. By contrast, Jesus directs our eyes to the point where everything is revealed. But we have to want to see it.

Second, the Jerusalem authorities failed to see by shutting their eyes to evidence that might have swayed them. Like most of us, they see only what they want to see and hear only what they want to hear. This selective seeing and hearing limits what we are able to understand of reality. Often, it even squeezes God out of the picture.

What About Me?

• *Seeing life through new eyes.* Have you ever spent fruitless minutes—or even hours—trying to match a jigsaw puzzle piece to its place in the picture only to find, after taking a short break, that it practically jumps into place? You realized you were looking right at it before, but you just didn't see it.

Do you ever wonder if this scenario plays out in everyday life? What would it feel like to see things that Christ would have us see that are right in front us? What would it be like to become aware of our own blind spots so we could learn to overcome them?

• *Looking where the light is.* Most people are familiar with the joke about the man looking for his lost car keys in the middle of the night. A passerby sees him and asks, "What are you looking for?" "My keys," the man replies. "And this is where you think you lost them?" "No...not really, but this is where the light is." What does this story say about us when we look for God only in convenient places? What could we do this week to venture into new areas of faith, trusting that the light of Christ is more powerful than any darkness we might encounter?

• *Learning to live in darkness.* Most of us know someone who is blind. It is fascinating to me to observe how the blind adapt to a world that is designed for sighted people. The attitude of the Jewish authorities shows how well we become adapted to our own blindness. Can you think of times when you altered your perspective on something? What happened that made you look twice at something you thought you understood?

Resources

John E. Hull, "John," *The Broadman Bible Commentary*, vol. 9 (Nashville TN: Broadman, 1970).

Gail R. O'Day, "The Gospel of John: Introduction, Commentary, and Reflections," *The New Interpreter's Bible*, vol. 9 (Nashville TN: Abingdon, 1995).

E. Gene Rooney, *Amphorae: Metaphoric Techniques for Understanding, Enhancing, and Improving Your Self-Image* (Reynoldsburg OH: L.E.A.D. Consultants, 1993).

D. J. Wiseman, "Siloam," *The Illustrated Bible Dictionary*, part 3, ed. J. D. Douglas (Downers Grove IL: InterVarsity, 1980), 1452.

THE LIGHT
SHINES IN THE DARKNESS
John 1:1-5; 9:1-7, 35-41

Introduction

Near the beginning of Advent last year, I dreamed that there was a book of ancient wisdom, disguised as a self-help bestseller, sitting on the shelves of an obscure bookstore not far from a subway station in the Meatpacking District of the West Village in New York City. I made my way to Christopher Street, where I had heard the bookstore was located. The building lacked a sign, but I finally found the store. It was small and slightly messy, and a nice young woman was working behind the cash register. I asked her about the book, but I didn't tell her it was really a book of esoteric secrets, cleverly disguised as a pop psychology bestseller. She told me there was one copy left, but even though she and I both looked for it, we never found it. Reluctantly, I left the store without the wisdom I had sought.

Then I dreamed about my father, who died several years ago and who hardly ever appears in my dreams. He stood in the kitchen of my grandparents' house in Huntington, West Virginia. I was a young adult. He had tears and tenderness in his eyes. The words he tried to speak caught in his throat: "There's something I want to tell you, something you need to know." He never got past "something you need to know," and I woke up without having heard what he so urgently wanted me to hear.

I think a lot of people share the restlessness reflected in my dreams. We want to know the truth about life, about what it means to be human, and about God. During Advent this year, we will study John 1:1-18 and thematically related passages in the rest of John's Gospel. John's prologue is largely a hymn about Jesus. It declares him to be God's Word and wisdom. It discusses the meaning of creation, human nature, and the character of God. This crucial wisdom isn't hidden in a book we can't find, and it isn't a secret that died, unvoiced, with people who weren't able to teach us. There isn't a map or a key that we need to go looking for. John's prologue tells us that the wisdom and Word of God have come among us in Jesus.

Sources for John's Prologue: The Wisdom and Word of God

Fairly early in Christian history, the eagle became a symbol for John's Gospel. New Testament scholar Raymond Brown believed that the "celestial flights of the opening lines of the gospel" were largely the reason for this (*The Gospel According to John*, vol. 1 [Garden City NY: Doubleday, 1966] 29). Most scholars believe that this hymn existed prior to its inclusion in this Gospel. They speculate about whether the same author who wrote the rest of the Gospel composed it or whether the author borrowed it from another source. There are other early hymns about Christ in the New Testament, most notably Philippians 2:5-11 and Colossians 1:15-20. John's prologue interrupts the hymn at a few points with explanations and interpretations written in prose (vv. 6-8, 13, 15).

Jewish texts about wisdom, personified as a woman, helped to shape the prologue. Proverbs 8:1-4 and 22-30 are most prominent, but Job 28 expands upon the same themes, as do apocryphal texts such as Sirach 1:1-9, 24:1-17; Wisdom 8:3, 9:4; and Baruch 3:10-13, 29-36. Like the Word of God in John's Gospel, "Lady Wisdom" was present with God before anything else came into existence: "The Lord created me at the beginning of his way, before his deeds long in the past. I was formed in ancient times, at the beginning, before the earth was.... I was there when he established the heavens, when he marked out the horizon on the deep sea" (Prov 8:22-23, 27). This feminine figure of Wisdom informs and interprets the prologue's description of Jesus as God's eternal Word.

In the background of this hymn there is also the richly meaningful idea of the Word (Greek, *logos*) of God. In the sixth century bc, Heraclitus of Ephesus described the *logos* as "the omnipresent wisdom by which all things are steered" (quoted by Leon Morris, *The Gospel According to John*, rev. ed. [Grand Rapids MI: Eerdmans,

1995] 102). Philo, an Alexandrian Jew, who was roughly a contemporary of the writer of John's Gospel, referred to the *logos* more than 1,200 times in his writings. George R. Beasley-Murray says that, for Philo, the *logos* was "the agent of creation, medium of divine government, the means of knowing God, and identified with perfect man" (*John* [Waco TX: Word, 1987] 6).

When John says, "The Word became flesh and made his home among us" (John 1:14), he is describing how God's *wisdom*, which was woven intimately into the fabric of creation and personified as a human being, and God's creative and transcendent *word*, which caused the world and its creatures to leap into existence, took on human flesh and lived among us in the person of Jesus.

In the Beginning

I am intrigued by how writers begin their stories, by how they say, "Once upon a time." There's no terser or more cosmic "Once upon a time" than the one the book of Genesis and the Gospel of John share in common. Genesis 1:1 says, "In the beginning, God created the heavens and the earth" (CEB margin) and John 1:1 says, "In the beginning was the Word."

John purposefully echoes Genesis. Genesis 1 tells us that God made the world by speaking; God created by means of God's Word: "God said, 'Let there be light.' And so light appeared" (Gen 1:3). John 1 tells us that "In the beginning was the Word.... What came into being through the Word was life, and the life was the light for all people" (John 1:1, 3-4).

God's Life and Light

John 1:1-5 claims that Jesus is the source and goal of creation. He is the alpha and the omega of the cosmos. The eternal Word is the energy and coherence of the universe, and this light shines in every place and on everyone, without condition or limitation.

Those themes are profound mysteries, laden with more meaning than we will be able to unpack in this single lesson. The main truth I want to underscore today is that we see God's life and God's light in Jesus. He shined and shines with the abundant and radiant life God wants us to experience.

In an interview with *Newsweek* magazine some years ago, the gritty and bluesy singer Lucinda Williams said,

> What happened to the rebellious nature of music and art? Van Gogh and those guys back then were temperamental and moody, but so what?... What happened to passion? Conviction? My friend says it would have been worse to have been born in Van Gogh's time. People died so young and all. I say, yeah, but at least they lived before they died. (Lorraine Ali, "Lucinda Straight Up," Newsweek, June 11, 2001, 55)

With Jesus, we get to live before we die because his hope is our fuel, his joy is our energy, and his love is our power. Nothing can quench the vitality or short-circuit the current of authentic life that courses through Jesus and flows into us. Darkness cannot defeat light. As John said, "The light shines in the darkness, and the darkness doesn't extinguish the light" (1:5).

Healed of Blindness by the Light of the World (9:1-7, 35-41)

The story from John 9 is about a beggar who had been born blind and to whom Jesus gave the gift of sight. This beggar had never gazed into his mother's eyes, observed his father's hands, saw a dog wag its tail, or beheld the glories of the Jerusalem temple in front of which he was consigned to beg.

Day by day, he did the only thing he could do to sustain his meager life: he called out to unseen passersby and pleaded with them to drop a coin or two in his basket. One day, he heard the footsteps of a group of people who drew near him and then stopped in front of him. No one spoke directly to him at first, but he heard one of Jesus' disciples ask, "Rabbi, who sinned so that he was born blind, this man or his parents?" (John 9:2).

Jesus' friends sound like insensitive medical students on rounds who are prone to forget that "the case" in front of them is not just a body with a disease, but a person with dignity and feelings—not the myocardial infarction in room 490, but Miriam, who has a broken heart. To them, he was little more than a flesh-and-bone question mark, an object of speculation.

Jesus' disciples assumed that this man's blindness was due to someone's badness. They thought that someone's sins, either his own or his parents', had robbed him of his sight. In that culture, people thought serious illnesses and handicaps were punishment. Suffering was deserved. Individuals or their families brought it on themselves.

Jesus was not interested in assigning blame, however, only in showing mercy. He didn't want to debate the cause of the man's blindness, only to offer compassion to him. Jesus dismissed his disciple's question as misguided. He said: "Neither he nor his parents. This happened so that God's mighty works might be displayed in him. While it's daytime, we must do the works of him who sent me. Night is coming when no one can work. While I am in the world, I am the light of the world" (9:3-5).

I'd prefer to punctuate the Common English Bible's translation in this way: "Neither he nor his parents. This happened. So that God's mighty works might be displayed in him, while it is daytime...." With this version of the punctuation, we are not left with the impression that God allowed the man to be born blind simply so he could see and celebrate Jesus' healing power. With this alternative punctuation there is no speculation about the cause of the blindness. Instead, there is a simple and stark acknowledgement: "This happened." We do not know with any certainty the reasons for his suffering.

The blind man felt warm mud on his eyes, and he heard Jesus say to him: "Go, wash in the pool of Siloam" (9:7). Something about Jesus caused him to obey. "He went away and washed," John writes. "When he returned, he could see" (9:7). As a consequence, he came to believe in Jesus as "the Human One" (9:35), the Son of Man, and he worshipped Jesus (9:38).

We are this blind beggar. Jesus has touched us, spoken to us, and instructed us. We trusted him, responded to him, and washed in the waters of obedience. He makes us able to see. He gives us insight into his identity and the meaning of our lives. With the blind man, we say, "I was blind and now I see" (9:25).

Because the shining light of the world restored our sight, we can see what we missed before. Before, life looked bland, dull, and ordinary. Now, we see that life itself shimmers with extraordinary wonder like a burning bush aflame with the presence of God. Before, we saw other people as strangers to fear and competitors to best. Now, we see them as neighbors to serve and companions with whom to share friendship. Before, we feared that we lived in a cold and empty universe. Now, we see that it is filled with the light and warmth of God's love. Before, we could see only the dark. Now, we see Jesus.

In Jesus is life, and he is the light for all people (John 1:4). He shines with the fullness of life that God intends for us to experience. Jesus also heals our spiritual blindness, so that we may see God, the world, ourselves, and other people more clearly than we've ever seen them before.

Notes

Notes

JOHN'S
TESTIMONY
John 1:6-9; 3:25-30

Central Question

What in my life is in competition with Jesus?

Scripture

John 1:6-9

1:6 A man named John was sent from God. 7 He came as a witness to testify concerning the light, so that through him everyone would believe in the light. 8 He himself wasn't the light, but his mission was to testify concerning the light. 9 The true light that shines on all people was coming into the world.

John 3:25-30

25 A debate started between John's disciples and a certain Jew about cleansing rituals. 26 They came to John and said, "Rabbi, look! The man who was with you across the Jordan, the one about whom you testified, is baptizing and everyone is flocking to him." 27 John replied, "No one can receive anything unless it is given from heaven. 28 You yourselves can testify that I said that I'm not the Christ but that I'm the one sent before him. 29 The groom is the one who is getting married. The friend of the groom stands close by and, when he hears him, is overjoyed at the groom's voice. Therefore, my joy is now complete. 30 He must increase and I must decrease."

Reflecting

I remember well an experience I had when I was a young boy. During a trip in the mountains of North Carolina with my parents, we stopped at a little store for a snack. This store enticed people to stop by way of a huge sign on the side of the road. In big bold letters the sign proclaimed, "The Most Photographed View in the Smoky Mountains."

While my parents and I were looking at souvenirs and enjoying being out of the car for a while, a tour bus stopped and parked next to the big sign. I watched as the passengers disembarked. What I saw next so totally overwhelmed me that the image is as real today as it was when I experienced it so many years ago.

This is what I observed: about twenty camera-wielding tourists scrambled off the bus. With lens caps flying and people elbowing one another to get into the perfect position, they all took their perfect picture...of the sign. They then filed back onto the bus. I vividly remember thinking to myself the caption for this scene that unfolded before me: *they saw the sign, but they missed the view.*

Today's Scripture passage explores John the Baptist's precarious situation. Like that sign proclaiming the magnificent view of the mountains, God had given John the task of getting the attention of God's people and announcing to them that the long-awaited Messiah was coming. In order to do this, John had to be bold. He had to attract a lot of attention and even be provocative. However, at the same time, John had to be transparent so that the bold sign would not obscure the view it was proclaiming.

> Why do some Christians seem more interested in following a popular pastor or other religious leader than they are in following Christ?

It is the second Sunday of Advent. Christmas shopping is at a frenzied pace. Television and print ads are all proclaiming Christmas gift ideas. The streets and houses are dressed in colored lights. The story of John the Baptist helps us remember that the hype is so big because the coming of Jesus is so important. But his story also calls us to remember that the signs of the season should never get in the way of our view of our Savior.

Studying

Introducing John the Baptist. History knows him as John the Baptist. If we had only the Gospel of John to describe this pivotal person, however, he might well have been known today as John the Witness or perhaps John the Proclaimer. Many of the familiar details of John's ministry are absent from the Fourth Gospel: his family connection to Jesus, his unique clothing and diet, and even the fiery nature of his preaching.

The author of the Fourth Gospel acknowledges John the Baptist's ministry of baptizing, but he doesn't dwell on it. Furthermore, nothing at all is said about his role in baptizing Jesus (see Matt 3:13-17; Mark 1:9-11; Luke 3:21-22). The Baptist's introduction in the prologue and the further description of his ministry in John 3 underscore his ministry of proclamation far beyond his role as baptizer.

Last week, the poetic nature of John's prologue (1:1-18) was discussed. The verses that introduce John (vv. 6-8) seem to be insertions to elaborate on the theme of light developed in the verses immediately before and after.

Although the writer maintains his economy of words, there is a stark contrast of language between his description of John and his description of Jesus. The abrupt change of tone gives the reader a clear sense of transition in the flow of ideas. In verses 1-5, we see that Jesus is eternal and intimately connected to the God of creation. By contrast, verses 6-8 show us that John is only a man—yet is at the same time a man who has been sent by God with a prophetic mission.

The Gospel writer lays John's task before the reader in verse 7. His only assignment is to give testimony of Jesus, the light. He then repeats this important distinction between John, the

proclaimer, and Jesus, the one being proclaimed (v. 8). Elsewhere in Scripture, there are references to people continuing to follow John long after Jesus came on the scene (see Acts 19:1-7). There may well have been rivalry between the two factions that the Gospel writer needed to address. At any rate, both here and in chapter 3, John's subordinate position is made abundantly clear.

We would need to examine the other three Gospels for a more complete view of John and his ministry. Here, the key idea is simply the relationship between the messenger and the message.

John and Jesus. John 3:25-30 gives us a hint at the rivalry that existed between followers of John and followers of Jesus. The tensions between these two groups were on the rise. Someone, no doubt one of his own followers, notes that Jesus had begun his own ministry of baptizing—and that people were flocking to him.

The practice of baptism by Jesus and his disciples is mentioned nowhere else in the four Gospels. Here, it is a source of contention between his group and that of John the Baptist. Both groups are obviously quite similar to each other in message and methods. This similarity brings rivalry, and this rivalry now reaches the boiling point.

A debate arises between John's disciples and a person identified only as "a certain Jew" (John 3:25). This statement hints at several possible issues that may have been circulating at the time. Perhaps the debate was over the meaning of the baptism John performed. There certainly could have been some confusion over the ways in which his baptism was similar to or different from the various cleansing rituals with which the Jews were familiar. Or perhaps the debate had to do with differences between those who had been baptized by John and those who had been baptized by Jesus' disciples. Did the two baptisms mean the same thing? Did one baptism have greater merit than the other? And if so, whose was best?

When his followers brought this debate to John, his heart must have sunk. John refuses to criticize those who are flocking to Jesus. Rather, he says that people are coming to Jesus because of God's blessing: "No one can receive anything unless it is given from heaven" (John 3:27). I can just hear John speaking in a dejected voice, with his head in his hands as he reminds his supporters of what they surely must already know, that John's mission was to announce the coming of the Messiah—and that was certainly not him (v. 28).

The parable that follows is another attempt to bring this point home (v. 29). John's followers knew about wedding customs. Perhaps they could identify with the feelings of a happy best man. Surely they had seen how the friends of both the bride and groom experience the joy of the occasion—not because they themselves are getting married but because they share in the joy of the ones they love.

> No man will make a great leader who wants to do it all himself or get all the credit for doing it.

This imagery drives home the meaning of John's words in verse 30: "He must increase and I must decrease." Like the attendants in a wedding photo, John doesn't have to be front and center; he is content to remain in the background. He doesn't have to be the focus of attention in order to experience the joy of simply being present and having a small role to play.

In the Fourth Gospel, every mention of John the Baptist is briefer than the one before until he at last passes completely from the scene. This encounter in chapter 3 marks the end of John's ministry in the Fourth Gospel. He has done well. He has captured the people's attention, but now he selflessly moves out of the way so the one he was proclaiming can take center stage.

John's followers seemed inclined to count numbers to see who was "winning." John, however, kept score in a totally different way. He understood that to win, he must lose in the conventional sense. This also proved to be the way of the Christ he proclaimed.

Understanding

Although there are many ways to view these passages, two in particular seem most helpful. First, we can ask what these passages teach us when we look at them from the perspective of John the Baptist. Second, we can explore what we learn when we assume the vantage point of those who heard John's preaching.

John the Baptist is clearly a worthy model of a life of witness to Christ. First, he was bold in his faith. He did not shy away from the discipline needed to both proclaim the reality of Jesus and to live a life that reflected his faith in Jesus. Second, although he was in many ways a larger-than-life character, he was willing and able to get out of the way so that the one he proclaimed would be the focus. Third, he did not fall into the trap of sectarian or personal competitiveness. He kept a completely different scorecard from those who took offense at Jesus' growing popularity. He was confident enough in his calling to let Jesus "increase" even as he himself "decreased" (John 3:30).

Thinking about these passages from the perspective of those who heard John, one can come away with a different set of insights. First, the followers of John show us how easy it is to get caught up in the glitz and glamour of a charismatic messenger and totally miss the message. This is of real concern in this season of the year, as the meaning of Christmas tends to get lost in hyper-consumerism. Second, we must be vigilant that we do not fall into competitions that only diminish the work of the church. By keeping the focus on Christ, the differences between congregations and denominations take on a much lower priority. Perhaps we could all benefit from the view that Jesus must increase and I—or my congregation or my denomination—must decrease.

What About Me?

• *The economy of scarcity.* Apparently, the followers of John the Baptist believed in "the economy of scarcity," the assumption that the more I give to you, the less I will have for myself. John therefore explained his relationship to Jesus in terms his disciples could understand: "He must increase and I must decrease" (3:30). It is clear, however, that John felt no defeat in this. On the contrary, such "decrease" was the culmination of his work. What would it take for us to embrace John's attitude and suffer "decrease" so that Christ and his kingdom could "increase" in our midst?

• *The importance of "brownie points."* A retired missionary once told me, "In ministry, just about anything can happen so long as no one tries to take the credit." In our culture, we have come to expect a reward to follow every good deed. What would it be like for us to do something good and not worry about being praised for it? Could we behave that sacrificially? Whom do you know who lets others shine by remaining in the background?

• *How do we see Jesus?* We live in a media-dominated culture. We want instant, continuous access to information. How does the message of Jesus compete in such a media-saturated world? How do the technological advances of our day both help and hinder our ability to see and hear Christ? What aspects of our fast-paced world compete with Jesus and his cause?

• *The transparent sign.* The lesson began with a story about the sign that distracted tourists from the view of the mountains. John shows us that the best sign is the one that can become transparent. Such a sign beckons us to see the view beyond the sign itself. What are the obstacles that keep us from pointing people to Jesus? How can we become more intentional and yet transparent in our witness of Christ?

Resource

J. Bradley Chance, "John the Baptist," *Mercer Dictionary of the Bible*, ed. Watson E. Mills (Macon GA: Mercer University Press, 1990), 459.

John's
Testimony
John 1:6-9; 3:25-30

Vulnerability and Authentic Witness

Thanks to Facebook, Twitter, and YouTube, I know a lot more than I ever thought I would about what people eat, where they go, the songs they like, the TV shows they watch, the tricks their pets do, how they vote, their blood pressure, the distance they ran or walked or rode their bikes, and whether or not they are having a good hair day. I know when friends check in at the airport, see pictures of the food they order in fancy restaurants, and get real-time reviews of the movies they are watching.

I think it's ironic that we have instant access to endless details about each other, but we still don't truly know each other. I can know what you had for breakfast, but not the dreams and hopes that get you up in the morning. I can know what you watched on late-night television, but not the fears that keep you awake at night. I can know what kind of coffee you like, but not what energizes you. I can know how you spend your time, but still be unsure how you are investing your life.

We don't necessarily know each other, because what we lack are vital experiences of face-to-face, eye-to-eye, and heart-to-heart vulnerability. Vulnerability connects us to each other.

Vulnerability frightens us, though. We're not sure we're willing to risk the hurt it might bring. We shield ourselves from the pain of it, not realizing that the shield against disappointment and hurt is also a barrier against love and joy. What we need is to press past our understandable resistance and live with radical openness to the wonders and wounds of life and with a spirit of generous welcome to all people in their marvel and messiness.

Vulnerability is the heart of all faithful witness. We take most seriously the perspectives and viewpoints of people who bear the marks of authenticity. We pay closest attention to people who are clearly speaking from their own experience and not parroting someone else. We take notice when it's evident that what people say and do cost them something. We want to know that they have skin in the game that they're trying to get us to play.

If my faith doesn't reorder my priorities and rearrange my schedule, affect where my money goes, pry open my heart to the beauty and pain of the world, and make me more compassionate for the broken and more passionate for justice and peace, then it isn't worth anyone else's consideration. If there's nothing at stake for me, it won't make any difference to you.

John the Baptist: A Vulnerable and Faithful Witness to Jesus

John the Baptist was a vulnerable and faithful witness to Jesus. He wasn't vulnerable in any conventional sense. We know from the Synoptic Gospels that John was formidable and off-putting for many people (see Mark 1:4-8; Matthew 3:1-12; Luke 3:1-17). He wore strange clothes: a camel-hair robe cinched in place with a leather belt. He ate an odd diet: locusts and wild honey. He lived in the wilderness, near the river. His voice often sounded more like thunder and lightning than it did like gentle rain. He said hard things in a hard way. He offered more challenge than comfort.

John was a slightly older member of Jesus' extended family, and he was a mentor and model to Jesus. His influence helped to shape how Jesus viewed himself, the world, and the coming kingdom of God. Jesus said publicly how much he admired John: "I assure you that no one who has ever been born is greater than John the Baptist" (Matt 11:11). Jesus praised John's strength: he wasn't a reed swayed by the wind, but a mighty oak of righteousness. Nor was he a trim and tapered candle that the slightest breeze could extinguish. Instead, he was a wildfire ablaze with the holy (Matt 11:7-8). The first sermon Jesus preached was an echo of the message he had heard John announce: "Change your hearts and lives! Here comes the kingdom of heaven!" (Matt 3:2).

Jesus and John were very different from each other. John was usually serious and stern while Jesus was most often tender and compassionate. John was the "bad cop" of judgment and Jesus was the "good cop" of grace. People criticized John for being no fun at all at a party. If he even showed up, he would sulk silently in the corner, refusing to dance and eating his strange, meager diet. By contrast, those same people accused Jesus of being the life of every party he attended. He enjoyed far too much the company of low-life sinners and eating and drinking everything in sight. They even called him a glutton and a drunkard (Matt 11:16-19).

Despite all the angles and hard edges to his personality, I think of John as a vulnerable and faithful witness because he yielded himself always to Jesus and to Jesus' vision of God and God's ways. We read in the first prose section of the prologue to John's Gospel that "a man named John was sent from God. He came as a witness to testify concerning the light, so that through him everyone would believe in the light. He himself wasn't the light, but his mission was to testify concerning the light" (John 1:6-8).

John's life had purpose because God sent him. His sense of calling assured him that who he was and what he did mattered. He especially knew that his identity and worth derived most significantly from his devotion to Jesus. John realized humbly and gratefully that he was not the light, but a reflection of it. He was not its source but its servant, not its origin but its witness.

Later in John 1, we find this important exchange between John and religious leaders from Jerusalem:

This is John's testimony when the Jewish leaders in Jerusalem sent priests and Levites to ask him, "Who are you?" John confessed (he didn't deny but confessed), "I'm not the Christ." They asked him, "Then who are you? Are you Elijah?" John said, "I'm not." "Are you the prophet?" John answered, "No." They asked, "Who are you? We need to give an answer to those who sent us. What do you say about yourself?" John replied, "*I am a voice crying out in the wilderness, Make the Lord's path straight*, just as the prophet Isaiah said." (1:19-23)

"Who are you?" the religious leaders wondered. John's answer is a wise claim of both importance and humility: "I am a voice" (v. 23)—not less, and not more, than a voice on behalf of Jesus. The life of a vulnerable and faithful witness makes sense only in connection with Jesus. A witness gives voice to another's truth by describing how that truth is changing and reordering his or her own life.

Our text from John 3 recounts a conversation between John and his disciples. They are concerned that Jesus is gaining such a large following. The Baptist responds by explaining that this is as it should be. John takes joy in seeing Jesus's ministry thrive. Jesus, in fact, must increase while John must decrease.

It's clear to me that John's disciples referred to Jesus when they said "The man who was with you across the Jordan," since they also said that this man was "the one about whom you testified" (John 3:26). It is, though, a curious way for them to describe someone so important to their teacher.

The references in John 3 (vv. 22, 26) to Jesus' baptizing others are intriguing. They seem to be in some tension with the statement in John 4:1-2 that "Jesus learned that the Pharisees had heard that he was making more disciples and baptizing more than John (although Jesus' disciples were baptizing, not Jesus himself)." Though it's possible that Jesus himself baptized people who came to him, it's most likely that Jesus "baptized" in the sense that he oversaw his disciples' baptism of others. Probably, those baptisms bore similar meaning as those conducted by John. They were enacted symbols of repentance in preparation for the coming kingdom of God.

The main point of John 3:25-30 has to do with the humility John brought to his vocation as a witness to Jesus. He confesses, "He must increase and I must decrease" (v. 30). John gladly points beyond himself to Jesus. Raymond Brown noted this interesting feature of the liturgical and astronomical calendars:

Just as the birthday of Jesus was fixed at December 25, the time of the winter solstice, after which the days grow longer (the light has come into the world; he must increase), so John the Baptist's birthday was fixed at June 24, the time of the summer solstice, after which the days grow shorter (he was not the light; he must decrease). The two Greek verbs in vs. 30 are also used for the waxing and waning of the light of heavenly bodies. (*The Gospel According to John*, vol. 1 [Garden City NY: Doubleday, 1966] 153)

"He must increase and I must decrease" was John's attitude toward Jesus. It can and should be our attitude as well. We may and must become more and more like Jesus. In the process, those dimensions of ourselves that aren't like him diminish. Whatever doesn't reflect his light fades away. He becomes greater in us.

Isaac of Stella, a twelfth-century Cistercian monk, prayed:

Let the Son of God grow in thee,
for he is formed in thee,
let him become immense in thee,
and may he become a great smile
and exultation and perfect joy. (quoted in Esther de Waal, *Lost in Wonder: Rediscovering the Spiritual Art of Attentiveness* [Collegeville MN: Liturgical Press, 2013] 43)

As Jesus increases in us—as he becomes immense in us—we are able to bear honest and vulnerable witness to him. We bear credibility to the extent that we live and talk like him and, I think, to the degree that we embody his "great smile and exultation and perfect joy."

We tell about our experience. I heard once about a Sunday school class that was studying the story in John's Gospel about Jesus' turning water into wine at a wedding feast. One fellow in the class was skeptical that it ever happened. He said, "Do you all really believe this? Why would Jesus turn water into wine? And how could he do it? It just doesn't make sense."

Another fellow in the class, a recovering alcoholic who had once spent his family into bankruptcy by wasting his money on booze, said, "I'll grant you it's a hard story, and I don't know how Jesus turned water into wine, but I can tell you this much: at my house, he turned beer into furniture" (William Barclay, *The New Daily Study Bible: The Letters to the Corinthians* [Louisville KY:

Westminster John Knox, 2002] 30). Merely relating the facts of a Bible story—Jesus turned water into wine—is not bearing witness. It is only a transfer of information. Witnessing is more like "At my house, he turned beer into furniture."

As witnesses, we don't try to answer every possible question or to explain mysteries beyond our power to understand. We simply tell stories about our own experience with Jesus. We tell of the grace we've experienced. We play the music that we've heard. We give the gifts we've received. We speak what we know, and we freely admit what we don't. Most of all, we offer our love. Because, day by day, people will turn to Jesus, not because of arguments we make, but because of the love we share.

Notes

Notes

JESUS' MISSION TO THE WORLD
John 1:10-13; 7:37-44

Central Question

What do I say about Jesus?

Scripture

John 1:10-13

10 The light was in the world, and the world came into being through the light, but the world didn't recognize the light. 11 The light came to his own people, and his own people didn't welcome him. 12 But those who did welcome him, those who believed in his name, he authorized to become God's children, 13 born not from blood nor from human desire or passion, but born from God.

John 7:37-44

37 On the last and most important day of the festival, Jesus stood up and shouted, "All who are thirsty should come to me! 38 All who believe in me should drink! As the scriptures said concerning me, *"Rivers of living water will flow out from within him."* 39 Jesus said this concerning the Spirit. Those who believed in him would soon receive the Spirit, but they hadn't experienced the Spirit yet since Jesus hadn't yet been glorified. 40 When some in the crowd heard these words, they said, "This man is truly the prophet." 41 Others said, "He's the Christ." But others said, "The Christ can't come from Galilee, can he? 42 Didn't the scripture say that the Christ comes from David's family and from Bethlehem, David's village?" 43 So the crowd was divided over Jesus. 44 Some wanted to arrest him, but no one grabbed him.

Reflecting

In the years I practiced pastoral counseling in North Carolina, I met many people who found themselves addicted to a variety of drugs, including alcohol. The collective themes of their stories will shed light on the Scripture passage that is the focus of this lesson.

The lives of those who succumb to drug addiction often follow similar trajectories. Experimental use becomes more frequent until the newly addicted person must use, not to get high, but to maintain a "normal." This inevitably leads to a series of bad choices that result in family, job, and other relational failures. The stories of addicts never fail to move me, as they allow me to see how ordinary people can slide down a slippery slope of bad choices.

Many of these people, having bottomed out, found a way back into physical and spiritual health through their faith. In the privacy of my counseling office, these people expressed to me some of the most powerful testimonies of what faith in Christ can do to reshape and redeem a lost life.

As I sought the meaning underlying these stories, a statement emerged that informed my counseling and my ministry: it's not all the things you get wrong in this world that really matter. What really matters is the *one thing* that you get right.

Each of us encounters countless choices every day. One choice we may hardly think about in our busy lives is this: who is Christ in my life today? Of all the choices we must make in a day, none is more important than this one for us to get right.

Today's Scripture passage speaks of the difficulty people had in Jesus' time understanding who he was and what his life and ministry meant. It was not easy to see Jesus clearly through the filters of the culture and philosophies of the time. Those who got it right found themselves caught in power struggles with the religious establishment. By giving the people the opportunity to decide who he was, Jesus created divisions that we still see today.

Studying

He Came to His Own. I hope you are becoming familiar with the format of the lessons in this unit. Each lesson is divided into two parts: a passage from the Johannine prologue and a complementary passage from later chapters of John. In today's first passage, John expands upon the metaphor of light to help us understand the nature of what Jesus brought to humanity. The second passage is an episode in which Jesus places himself alongside and even superior to Moses. We then see how the people reacted to Jesus' words and deeds and the resulting division their responses caused.

John 1:10-13 shows us God's desire for an intimate relationship with humanity through Jesus. Jesus, "the light" (v. 10), was intricately involved in the creation of the world and of the human race. Even so, people did not recognize him when he appeared among them or understand his mission or message.

To further the sense of divine disappointment over our failure to recognize Jesus, verse 11 brings the situation closer to home. By suggesting that even "his own" did not welcome him, John makes clear to his Jewish readers that they, above all the rest of the world, should recognize who Jesus was. After all, they were steeped in the biblical tradition. They should have understood what Jesus was about, but they didn't—even when Jesus stood right in front of them.

William Hull suggests reasons the people of Jesus' time failed to see in him the full manifestation of God in their midst. It would be helpful to explore what it would have meant to both Greeks and Jews to "welcome" or to receive Jesus.

Hull suggests that the Gentiles had difficulty in this regard because Jesus did not espouse a philosophy they could follow (216). There was no logical progression that led a person to understand the meaning of Jesus. It wasn't a pure mental exercise; the encounter with Jesus himself would have to be sufficient to receive or welcome him.

The Jews had their own problems in recognizing and welcoming Jesus. Of course, Jesus did not meet wide expectations of a military commander who would, like David, defeat Israel's enemies and bring the promised land back under Jewish control.

Nor did Jesus act like the expected Messiah in religious terms. The popular belief was that the Messiah would come as an authoritative interpreter of the law of Moses, clarifying issues of proper religious observance within the regulations of the Torah. While it could be argued that Jesus did, in fact, bring a fresh interpretation of the law, his message was more about inward transformation than outward conformity to religious rules. With Jesus, there was no list of rules to check off, and this made it harder for many Jews to receive his message.

Verses 12-13 speak of the promise of what will come to those who recognize and welcome Jesus into their lives. Such people become part of a family, brothers and sisters whose common Father is God. This new relationship to God and to one another is further defined in terms that differentiate it from anything that has been encountered before. It is not founded on human emotions or desires, nor does the relationship with God follow their more familiar notions of bloodlines. The relationship makes one "a child of God." God initiates and defines this relationship apart from any human input.

The Feast of Tabernacles. John 7 relates an incident that happened during the feast of Tabernacles. For seven days, the people of Jerusalem took part in a festival that recalled the miraculous provision of God as the ancient Israelites wandered in the wilderness on their way out of slavery and to the promised land. The provision of water was especially important, as it was impossible to survive

The feast of Tabernacles was one of Israel's three great annual festivals, celebrated with great joy in autumn, at the completion of the agricultural year. Its ancient purpose was to recall Israel's wilderness pilgrimage and, apparently, to enact a renewal of Israel's covenant with God.

The celebration lasted seven days, the first and last days being holy convocations. The people gathered in fruit and dwelled in booths made from branches and the boughs of trees. (Rylaarsdam, 455; Freeman, 505)

such a journey through the desert without it. The participants of the festival were reminded that God provided for their need by sending rain as well as bringing forth water from a rock when Moses struck it with his staff. The festival moved the participants

emotionally and spiritually into the awe their ancestors experienced in the book of Exodus.

On the last and greatest day of the celebration, Jesus calls those who are thirsty to come to him to drink. He claims the promise of life symbolized in the provision of water really springs from him (see John 4:13-14). Those who believe in him will find their spiritual thirst quenched and their hearts renewed.

Next, we hear the people's reaction to this provocative claim. As is usually the case in the Gospels, some try to understand Jesus in the familiar terms their tradition provided them. Perhaps he is a prophet, they say, or even the long-awaited Messiah.

Some, however, reject outright the possibility that Jesus could be the Messiah because of their assumptions about his origin. The Messiah could not come from Galilee, after all, but from Bethlehem (John 7:41-42). They did not know what Matthew and Luke report, that Jesus was, in fact, born in King David's hometown.

There was little middle ground with respect to Jesus and his identity. People were divided over him, and some even wanted to arrest him—a fact that highlights the vehemence of their rejection. Perhaps they saw in the passion of those who did believe how dangerous Jesus could be to their traditions and power structure. Then, as today, there is little middle ground in our relationship to Jesus.

Understanding

Who is Jesus to you? Would your simple affirmation that Jesus is Savior and Lord be so simple if it brought suspicion upon you? What if such an affirmation made you look disloyal to your faith and culture? Is being a Christian so easy today that it has lost its real meaning?

Perhaps it would be helpful if all Christians reevaluated what it means to "welcome" Christ. What does it mean to you, even on a daily basis, to be a believer, one who has embraced Jesus' call to serve God through him?

The addicts I mentioned at the beginning of this lesson often described Jesus as a powerful and transformative influence in their lives. But what about those whose life stories may not be so dramatic? Can Jesus make a real difference in more ordinary lives as well?

Today's Scripture passages invite us to ask these questions. How much of a difference we will allow Jesus to make in our lives?

In North America, being a Christian usually lets us blend into the background. Many people have found, however, that welcoming Jesus into their lives has made them stand out. Serving Christ can be dangerously controversial! Think of Clarence Jordan, Martin Luther King Jr., Dietrich Bonhoeffer, or Mother Teresa. Their welcome of Jesus into their lives and obedience to Jesus' commands inspired them to do extraordinary things. Some people consider them saints, but in their time, others thought of them as agitators and criminals—and some still do.

This is the effect Jesus had in the Gospels on those who encountered him. Today's texts invite us to consider what might happen when we submit to acting as the hands, feet, and voice of one who caused such a disturbance in his own time.

What About Me

• *Who is Jesus in my life today?* We often find ourselves becoming passive in our faith journey. It is easy to think about the time when we first accepted Christ into our hearts as both the beginning and the end of our contemplation of "Who is Jesus to me?" But this important question should lead us into a whole life of transformation. It is good to ask ourselves this question often. How will Jesus make a difference in my life today?

• *Making the tough choices.* Too often, we assume that peer pressure is strictly an issue for adolescents. In fact, it is something with which everyone struggles from time to time. Many people make decisions while calculating how their family, friends, colleagues, or neighbors might think of them. If we are honest with ourselves, we will conclude that following Christ often brings conflict with people to whom we are close. It is easy to say that we won't let those pressures hinder us, but is it the truth? How do we weigh the influence of those who matter to us the most?

• *Whose hand is on the wheel?* The people of Jesus' time measured his words against ancient traditions or philosophical approaches to life's great mysteries. It is easy for us to see how they let these old ways hinder their view of who Jesus was. We must also understand, however, that we, too, are influenced by powerful forces that shape our view of the world, such as politics, nationalism, economics, and the media, just to name a few. These influences shape the decisions we make every day. The season of Advent and the approaching new year are a good time to critically examine what influences our lives and how these influences might conflict with the voice of Christ.

Resources

D. Freeman, "Feasts," *The Illustrated Bible Dictionary*, Part 1, ed. J. D. Douglas (Downers Grove IL: InterVarsity, 1980).

John E. Hull, "John," *The Broadman Bible Commentary*, vol. 9 (Nashville TN: Broadman, 1970).

J. C. Rylaarsdam, "Feast of Booths," *The Interpreter's Dictionary of the Bible*, vol. 1, ed. George A. Buttrick (Nashville TN: Abingdon, 1962).

Jesus' Mission to the World
John 1:10-13; 7:37-44

Introduction

'Tis the season for too many parties offering us plentiful goodies, endless treats, and lavish delicacies. From years of going to these parties, I've learned that even though holiday foods don't have voices, they can nevertheless call our names. When they do, we're prepared to grant ourselves an indulgence in advance for overeating.

"Just this once," we tell ourselves. "Just tonight, just this bite, just a smidgen, just one more helping." I don't think we should feel bad about the feasting we do this time of year. After all, feasting was God's idea: the promised land flowed with milk and honey, a banquet table laden with rich foods is set for us in heaven, and Jesus turned water into abundant and delicious wine. When we enjoy festivals like Christmas with gratitude to God and gracious hospitality to one another, we're celebrating God's bounty and blessings.

Choosing against Life and Light

What would happen, though, if we ate all year like we eat at the Christmas party? What if we never opted for healthy foods in reasonable portion sizes? It would be like a woman on the verge of exhaustion who never learned to say "no" to another request for her help and never managed to say "yes" to a day off and a vacation. It would be like feeling out of touch with your children but never making time simply to hang out with them, listen to them, and learn what they care about.

It would be like cringing in the darkness of the shabby shack of fear when there's nothing besides our inertia to keep us from walking in the light of the world. It would be like surrendering to a halfhearted existence when nothing other than our resistance keeps us from experiencing the Life of all creation.

The prologue to John's Gospel acknowledges the disheartening truth that we sometimes choose against light and life. It begins with these inspiring words we read just a couple of weeks ago:

> In the beginning was the Word and the Word was with God and the Word was God. The Word was with God in the beginning. Everything came into being through the Word, and without the Word nothing came into being. What came into being through the Word was life, and the life was the light for all people. (John 1:1-5)

In Jesus, God's personal and powerful Word came into the world bringing light and life to all people. This is not the end of the story, however. In verses 10-13, John presents a vexing irony: the world did not recognize the Word that made it. The people whom the Word created did not welcome him.

Resisting and Refusing Jesus

John 7:37-44 recounts one of many incidents in the Fourth Gospel in which people who had an opportunity to recognize Jesus and receive what he offered them failed or refused to do so.

Jesus was among a throng of pilgrims who had gathered in Jerusalem to celebrate the Jewish Festival of Booths (or Tabernacles). It was autumn, just after harvest time. The mood at the festival was a great deal like the American Thanksgiving holiday. People expressed their gratitude and praise for the generous blessings God provided.

The pilgrims in Jerusalem camped out for eight days of worship and feasting. In fact, the festival derived its name from the temporary shelters or booths the pilgrims cobbled together in the outer courts of the temple and around the city. These makeshift shelters recalled and reenacted the wilderness wanderings of their ancestors on their way to the promised land.

God had been faithful in those days, providing manna from heaven and water from the rocks of the desert. The pilgrims who gathered for the Feast of Tabernacles affirmed that God continued to be faithful to them as well.

On most days of the festival, there were three joyful processions that included singing, flute-playing, and dancing. One of those processions went from the temple to the pool of Siloam and then back to the temple. From the pool, the priests drew large amounts of water. They brought this water with them as they led the procession back to the temple through the city's water gate. Once in the temple, the priests circled the altar with the water jars in their hands while the people sang "Hosannah, God save us." The priests poured the water around the altar as a sacrifice of praise and thanksgiving to God for the good and essential gift of water.

I am convinced that it was while the priests were pouring out this offering of water to God that Jesus stood up and shouted, "All who are thirsty should come to me! All who believe in me should drink! As the scriptures said concerning me, *Rivers of living water will flow out from within him*" (John 7:37-38).

John then adds this editorial comment: "Jesus said this concerning the Spirit. Those who believed in him would soon receive the Spirit, but they hadn't experienced the Spirit yet since Jesus hadn't yet been glorified" (v. 39).

With the words, "they hadn't experienced the Spirit yet," the Common English Bible is providing interpretation as much as, if not more than, translation. The New Revised Standard Version is more literal: "as yet the Spirit had not been given." I think the CEB's interpretation is correct, since, strictly speaking, there has never been a time when there was "no Spirit." John meant that the death and resurrection of Jesus undammed and set loose the river of the Spirit that would flow from Jesus into the heart of every disciple. The river of the Spirit courses through us with all the gifts and graces we need to live with authentic love and genuine joy.

Having heard Jesus offer these rivers of living water, people in the crowd of worshippers had varying reactions. Some thought he was the great prophet, one like Elijah, which their faith had taught them to expect in association with the coming of God's kingdom (Mal 4:5-6).

Some thought Jesus was the Messiah, the anointed liberator of God's people. Others doubted it was possible for Jesus, who was from the backwater town of Nazareth in Galilee, to be anyone extraordinary. They scoffed, "The Christ can't come from Galilee, can he?" (v. 41).

Referencing Micah 5, others asked, "Didn't the scripture say that the Christ comes from David's family and from Bethlehem, David's village?" (v. 42).

Of course, the readers of John's Gospel know what these skeptics did not (although they could have known it with only a modest amount of research). Jesus had, in fact, been born in Bethlehem, the city of David.

The skeptics couldn't be bothered, however, with finding out the simple facts about Jesus before forming their opinion of him. They and the people who disparaged Jesus because of his humble origins were captives of their own biases, stereotypes, and unteachable spirits. Light and life stood before them, but they clung to the status quo of their darkness and death. Their lack of openness to Jesus demonstrated what the prologue anticipated: "The light was in the world, and the world came into being through the light, but the world didn't recognize the light. The light came to his own people, and his own people didn't welcome him" (John 1:10-11).

I am not precisely sure why it is that we resist and refuse what is best for us—those things that would bring us light and give us real life—but I know we do. Steven Pressfield is the author of *The Legend of Bagger Vance* and other books. He is passionate about his writing, but he also is aware of his tendency to conspire against himself and allow others to sabotage his work. He calls this tendency "resistance." He describes it this way: "Resistance is directly proportional to love. If you're feeling massive Resistance, the good news is, it means there's tremendous love there too.... The opposite of love isn't hate; it's indifference" (*The War of Art* [New York: Black Irish, 2002] 42).

"Indifferent" is how I would characterize many people's response to Jesus. They certainly don't hate him. They respect his willingness to die for his commitments. They recognize his significance in human history. They value whatever they might know of his teachings, such as the Golden Rule or the Beatitudes. Most of the time, though, he simply isn't on their minds.

Even Jesus' followers can grow indifferent to him. We postpone the pursuit of life-giving commitments. We make excuses for clinging to the way things are rather than opening our hands to receive what could be. We rationalize our reluctance to admit we were wrong and receive forgiveness. We deflect responsibility for our part in becoming whole. We refuse Jesus' invitation to wonder and love even when we really want to say "yes." We don't intend our avoiding and delaying to be outright rejections of Jesus but the effect is the same. We've closed ourselves to him and the life and light he gives.

There wouldn't be resistance if there weren't love. If we can press through our resistance, Jesus will convince us that we are children of God: "Those who did welcome him, those who believed in his name, he authorized to become God's children, born not from blood nor from human desire or passion, but born from God" (John 1:12-13).

In this same Gospel, the first extended conversation Jesus has is with a religious leader named Nicodemus. Jesus intrigued Nicodemus. This untrained rabbi from Galilee had a quality of vitality and an air of freedom Nicodemus longed to experience.

Nicodemus asked Jesus, "Rabbi, we know that you are a teacher who has come from God, for no one could do these miraculous signs that you do unless God is with him" (John 3:2). His statement was a thinly disguised question: "Teacher, how can I know God the way you know God?"

Jesus answered, "I assure you, unless someone is born anew, it's not possible to see God's kingdom" (3:3). Jesus said, essentially, "No one can see what I see, feel what I feel, hear what I hear, and know what I know about God—unless he or she is born again, this time from above."

Nicodemus doubted it was possible. "How is it possible for an adult to be born?" he asks. "It's impossible to enter the mother's womb for a second time and be born, isn't it?" (3:4). Nicodemus had been around long enough to know what was possible and what was not. For him, transformation was at the top of the list of impossible things.

Jesus answered, "Whatever is born of the flesh is flesh, and whatever is born of the Spirit is spirit" (3:6). Notice how Jesus' words echo those of the prologue, where we read that God's children are "born not from blood nor from human desire or passion, but born from God" (1:13). The birth of new life does not depend on us but on God.

Jesus underscored the mystery of God's power to generate newness in us. He said, "Don't be surprised that I said to you, 'You must be born anew.' God's Spirit blows wherever it wishes. You hear its sound, but you don't know where it comes from or where it is going. It's the same with everyone who is born of the Spirit" (3:7-8).

The wind of God blows where it wills, sweeping us up and carrying us along. God's Spirit conceives new life in us just as God's Spirit brought Jesus to life, first in Mary's womb and then, through her, into the world itself. Because Jesus has been born into the world, because the Word of light and life has become flesh, you can be a new person—a child of God. It's a promise to all who receive, accept, and welcome Jesus.

Notes

Notes

4

THE WORD BECAME FLESH
John 1:14-18; 6:35-40

Central Question

How has heaven come to earth in Jesus?

Scripture

John 1:14-18

1:14 The Word became flesh and made his home among us. We have seen his glory, glory like that of a father's only son, full of grace and truth. 15 John testified about him, crying out, "This is the one of whom I said, 'He who comes after me is greater than me because he existed before me.'" 16 From his fullness we have all received grace upon grace; 17 as the Law was given through Moses, so grace and truth came into being through Jesus Christ. 18 No one has ever seen God. God the only Son, who is at the Father's side, has made God known.

John 6:35-40

6:35 Jesus replied, "I am the bread of life. Whoever comes to me will never go hungry, and whoever believes in me will never be thirsty. 36 But I told you that you have seen me and still don't believe. 37 Everyone whom the Father gives to me will come to me, and I won't send away anyone who comes to me. 38 I have come down from heaven not to do my will, but the will of him who sent me. 39 This is the will of the one who sent me, that I won't lose anything he has given me, but I will raise it up at the last day. 40 This is my Father's will: that all who see the Son and believe in him will have eternal life, and I will raise them up at the last day."

Reflecting

What if you just woke up from a coma-like sleep and didn't know what season of the year it was? A quick look at the television would soon give you clues. Going to town, to the mall, or even a grocery store would leave no doubt in your mind about the time of year and what is about to happen. Especially at night, with usually ordinary houses now aglow with multicolored lights, any doubt you might have had about the season of the year would be completely cast aside.

It is Christmas. Everything is adorned to remind us of that fact. Even if you had no access to a calendar, just look around. Seeing is believing.

At Christmas, we celebrate the birth of Jesus. More importantly, we also celebrate the meaning of Jesus' birth: that God has become flesh and blood.

Because God so reveals the glory of all God is through the person of Jesus Christ, we can look and see, we can listen and hear, and we can touch and feel the very mystery of God.

At the time of Jesus' coming, the Jewish people had already enjoyed a long history and tradition of God's interaction with them. God showed divine power and might through miraculous events. Plagues in Egypt led to liberation. Bread and quails sustained them on their wilderness journey. God was evident in the powerful words of the prophets as well as in God's divine guidance of the lives of Israel's ancient kings.

A person may hear the wind. Certainly one can see evidence of the wind in the movement of trees and grass. Such was the revelation of God before Christ: no one saw God, only the evidence of God. But with the coming of Christ, this relationship with God totally changed. Humanity was not only blessed with the movement of God's power in our midst, now we could see the wind directly.

> **?** Does getting into the "Christmas spirit" depend on the outward trappings of the season for you? How can we experience the wonder of Christmas when these external cues are missing?

Even so, the people of Jesus' time still asked him to "shake the tree" so they could recognize the signs they were accustomed to. They still had trouble seeing and believing.

Studying

The Word Has a Name. Christmas is less than a week away. In our study of John's prologue, we come at last to the one phrase of Scripture that best captures what this whole season is about: "The Word became flesh" (John 1:14). John's Gospel does not regale us with stories of wise men and shepherds, of angels and mangers. However, in these four words, John states in no uncertain terms the true substance of the Christmas story.

After having discussed the theme of "light" in some detail, John returns in verse 14 to the matter of the "Word," which has not been mentioned since verse 1. The first few verses of the Fourth Gospel speak about the preeminence, power, and light- and life-giving qualities of the Word. Now, we come to the Christmas moment itself, the time in which all of these qualities described so beautifully become flesh and mingle among us for a time.

What is eternal has now acquired a temporal character. God has become one of us so that we might see God with our eyes, hear God with our ears, and experience God with all our heart. Is it any wonder that we so love to celebrate Christmas?

The theological term for this mystery is "incarnation." The word comes from the Latin translation of John 1:14. The doctrine of the incarnation seeks to explain how the divine took bodily form in Christ. This is, in fact, central to the Christian faith. According to Don Olive, "That Jesus is God incarnate informs every tenet of the faith, from creation to eschatology. It particularly involves the doctrine of salvation, for the incarnation of God in Jesus remains the key for understanding how the estrangement between humans and God is remedied" (404).

The embodiment or incarnation of all that God is, as seen in and through the person and the life of Jesus Christ, becomes for Christians the primary way in which we can experience the glory of God. When people see the miraculous works of God, the Bible often says that such people have seen the glory of God. Do we grasp the glory of God that is evident in the birth of Christ?

Perhaps we have become so used to the Christmas story that this aspect of it is lost to us. If so, we must pay even closer attention to what John is saying. In all the history of God's interventions with human beings, the one act that best illuminates God's glory is God taking on the totality of human existence. The full extent of God's gracefulness and faithfulness is fully revealed in this event (v. 14).

What comes to us through this great gift of Christmas? What is the meaning of the "fullness" of what we have received? John answers this: "grace upon grace" (v. 16). Grace is stacked upon more grace. Christ gives us in boundless supply the richest of all of God's blessings, the grace that restores our souls.

John knew his audience well. Everyone reading his Gospel would have been intimately familiar with the way God used Moses to deliver the law (v. 17). This was unquestioned history and tradition. The Jews trusted this redeeming story above every other manifestation of God's relationship with them. Now, however, John introduces a new chapter in their history and traditions. He announces that it is time to turn the page and know that God is revealing God's self in a new, fuller, richer way.

The totality of God's grace and the ultimate embodiment of God's faithfulness have come into the world in a very special way. John has waited until this moment to finally give a name to this incarnation of God, the Word, the Light, the revealer of grace and truth, and his name is Jesus Christ (v. 17).

John must be clear at this point. Jesus is "God the only Son" (v. 18). Moses was great. John the Baptist did wonderful work. But Jesus is totally unique. There is no other like Jesus, and the most unique aspect of Jesus is his intimate relationship with the one God whom Jesus calls Father.

The Gift and the Giver. John 6 begins with the wonderful story of the feeding of the 5,000 from the meager meal of a young child. This story was a sign that Jesus himself had come to be the "bread of life" (John 6:35, 48).

There are two important aspects to the opening of Christmas presents: the gift itself and the giver of the gift. The incarnation rolls these two aspects into one. When people come to Jesus asking for more bread (John 6:34), Jesus declares, "I am the bread of life" (v. 35). He is not only the giver; he is the gift as well.

Finally, Jesus addresses the theme that runs throughout the Fourth Gospel. People saw with their own eyes the signs and the wonders of Jesus, but they failed to recognize what they were seeing. Perhaps it is too much tradition that clouds their vision— too much expectation of what the future may hold that actually hinders them from seeing what is in front of them.

Jesus could not be clearer in representing the heart of God. What he told the crowd should have softened even the most hardened heart. His message should ring as clearly as the Christmas bells heralding the Advent season: "This is my Father's will: that all who see the Son and believe in him will have eternal life" (John 6:40). Seeing is believing, or at least it is when we live within the will of our Father in heaven.

Christmas is such a special time. The grand expectancy of the Advent season finally gives way to the reality of Jesus in the flesh dwelling among us. But unlike the freshness of the new toys lying in wait to be opened, or the purity of the white snow that might bless some of us on Christmas morning, the promise of God through the gift of Christ is of an eternal nature. Christ's love is God's gift, which is promised to the end of time. It's Christmas! See, believe, and open the gift of unbridled hope for the future.

Understanding

Our 2,000-year retrospective view of the coming of Christ has both advantages and disadvantages. We did not actually get to see God incarnate with our own eyes. We did not get to hear his words with our own ears or even in our own language. A hundred generations have come and gone. In that amount of time, history has a way of growing murky. The memories of the eyewitnesses fade away.

But we have the advantage of a 2,000-year retrospective, as well. The incredible reality of God incarnate is difficult for us to fully embrace. It sounds like an impossibility, too incredible to be true. Yet for 2,000 years, we have grown to accept the incarnation as the gift that it is. For twenty centuries, we have come to know

God through the revelation of Christ. To be sure, it does take a while to grasp this great truth, but with our many years of reflection, we might take it for granted.

We read of those who had trouble seeing and believing and from our lofty perch we may wonder why it didn't come easier. We forget how new it was to them.

But we can learn a lesson from their difficulty. We have had twenty centuries to get used to the story, twenty centuries to grow unimpressed by the deeper meaning of Christ's coming.

We would all do well to emulate those who came before us by trying to see Jesus through their fresh eyes. Looking at the familiar story of Jesus' birth while seeking a deeper perspective on its meaning would be a helpful exercise this Christmas season.

New eyes may well bring a new vision of Christ, a vision that will open us to a new appreciation for an incredible and nearly unbelievable God.

What About Me

• *Incarnate grace.* We know the ultimate sacrifice that Christ made on our behalf on the cross, but the grace of God as seen through Christ was lived out every day of his ministry on earth. What were some of the ways Jesus exhibited grace to those he encountered along the way? Can we get in touch with that grace as we seek ways to feel God's redeeming power and as we exhibit a gracious spirit for other people? We have been taught to "forgive and forget." Try to remember a time when you felt forgiven and a time when you forgave. It is best to remember the joy of those occasions.

• *Incarnate truth.* We mostly associate truth with not telling falsehoods, and that is certainly an important part of it. But more foundationally, truth refers to faithfulness. It has a lot to do with living in covenant with one another. What promises do we keep every day? How important is this kind of truth in family relationships, in church relationships, or at work?

• *Incarnate glory.* The fullness or glory of God was seen in the face of Christ. Not in the heavens, but in his smile; not in mighty winds or earthquakes, but in a healing touch. The glory of God is seen in human form and you can be part of that incarnation. How can we serve others in a way that will show someone God's truth, grace, and glory?

Resource

Don H. Olive, "Incarnation," *Mercer Dictionary of the Bible*, ed. Watson E. Mills (Macon GA: Mercer University Press, 1990).

THE WORD
BECAME FLESH
John 1:14-18; 6:35-40

Introduction

The prologue of John's Gospel compresses the Christmas story into a single and shimmering sentence: "The Word became flesh and made his home among us. We have seen his glory, glory like that of a father's only son, full of grace and truth" (John 1:14). There are no anxious parents, singing angels, frightened shepherds, or worshipping wise men in this account. There isn't even a sleeping baby!

Instead, John goes straight for the meaning of Christmas: in Jesus of Nazareth, God became a human being. The God who made everything and everyone lived an individual life, in a particular place, and at a specific time. We know that idea—that God took on flesh and became a human being—as the *incarnation*.

The Embodiment of God

In Jesus, God took on the constraints and possibilities of a completely embodied life. Jesus had the night's chill cuddled away by Mary's tender embrace. He felt sheltered and safe in Joseph's strong arms. He laughed when Mary tickled his feet and shouted with glee when Joseph tossed him in the air. He skinned his knees when he was learning to walk. He hit his thumb with a hammer while working in Joseph's carpentry shop.

As a teenager, he felt stabs of desire when a pretty girl smiled at him. He had headaches, suffered indigestion, caught colds, and sweated through fevers. He knew the frustration of an occasional sleepless night, had leg cramps when he walked too long and too far, and knew how hard it is to be kind when you're worn out. He enjoyed food and wine, and also knew what it was like to be hungry and thirsty.

When Jesus died, his strength was beaten out of him, his wrists and ankles were ripped by nails and bound by ropes, and a crown of thorns was pressed on his head. A spear ripped open his side, and his blood oozed out of his body and flowed onto the ground.

Because the Word became flesh in Jesus, God experienced all these very human things. That is what the incarnation means. That is what Christians believe.

With his body, Jesus spoke and showed the good news of God's love for us. With his eyes, he saw the furrows of worry in people's faces, the tearstains on their cheeks, the downcast gazes, and the slumped shoulders, but also the dancing eyes, the bright smiles, the springing steps, and the outstretched arms. With his ears, he heard painful moans, lonely cries, and whispered questions, but also delightful laughter, songs of wonder, and shouts of praise.

On his feet, Jesus went to the marginalized and estranged. With his arms, he embraced outcasts and welcomed sinners. With his hands, he blessed children, restored sight to the blind, and broke bread for the hungry. On his knees, he washed the feet of his friends. With his mouth, he spoke words of challenge and comfort.

God's Self-Revelation in the Flesh of Jesus

In the flesh and blood of Jesus, the Word was in the world. Jesus is God's own answer to the question "What are you like?" In Jesus, we hear from God about God.

The writer of Hebrews put it this way: "In the past, God spoke through the prophets to our ancestors in many times and many ways. In these final days, though, he spoke to us through a Son. God made his Son the heir of everything and created the world through him. The Son is the light of God's glory and the imprint of God's being" (Heb 1:1-3).

Similarly, John 1:18 says, "No one has ever seen God. God the only Son, who is at the Father's side, has made God known."

Later in John's Gospel, Jesus says to one of his disciples, "Whoever has seen me has seen the Father" (John 14:9).

A glorious truth of Christmas is that God is like Jesus. One powerful dimension of that truth is that any image or concept of God, any feeling or conviction about God, or any claim or statement on God's behalf that is inconsistent with the character and spirit of Jesus is not a full or adequate understanding of God. Jesus is God's self-portrait. Jesus is what God says, what God does, and who God is.

Jesus makes it clear that God is not distant from us but, instead, is here with us. God dwells among us. God comes to us wherever we are. As Jesus told his friends, "I won't leave you as orphans. I will come to you" (John 14:18).

Jesus shows us that God is not vindictive and capricious, ready to pounce on us with harshness and punishment. Instead, God comes to us in our failures, lifts us out of guilt, wipes the tears of shame from our eyes, and tells us, as Jesus told the woman caught in the act of adultery, "Neither do I condemn you. Go, and from now on, don't sin anymore" (John 8:11).

The Bread of Life

God became flesh in Jesus so we can trust the goodness and love of God. God also became flesh so we can be sure that bodies—our bodies and the bodies of all other people—matter to God. Because God cares about bodies, God cares about food. The simple fact that there is a table and a meal at the heart of the church's worship means at the very least that God cares about tables and mealtimes and about who's included and who's left out.

God cares about the condition of the soil from which food grows, about the dignity and health of the farmers who grow it, about the fairness by which it is sold and marketed, and about the equity and justice of its distribution. God cares about people who don't have enough food, which is why Jesus so often fed hungry people. God also cares about people who struggle with food: people who have substituted it for love and can't get enough of it, even when they have eaten far too much. And God cares for people who are obsessed with controlling how much food they eat because they feel so out of control in other parts of their lives.

These struggles over food and its meaning remind us that bread is never just bread; it also is a sign and symbol of our deepest needs. Like the other Gospels, John tells us of a time when, to the amazement of all who saw him do it, Jesus fed thousands of hungry people in the desert by multiplying meager resources into an abundant feast (John 6:1-15).

As John remembered the story, a young boy offered Jesus five barley loaves and two fish—nearly nothing when compared to the hunger of the crowds gathered in the wilderness to hear Jesus teach. Jesus took those loaves of bread and those dried fish, gave thanks for them, and broke them again and again until well more than five thousand people had more than enough to eat. From next to nothing, Jesus brought such abundance that when the meal was over and everyone was satisfied, Jesus' friends collected twelve baskets of leftovers.

After that miracle skeptics and critics interrogated Jesus. They demanded to know how he did what he did and, even more importantly, they wanted to know who he really was. Jesus said, "I am the bread of life. Whoever comes to me will never go hungry, and whoever believes in me will never be thirsty" (John 6:35). God's care for our bodies is part of God's care for our whole selves, including our minds, emotions, and spirits.

God cares about the struggles we have with pain and disease. God is with us when we undergo cancer, chemotherapy, and radiation treatments; mastectomies and reconstruction; hip replacement, knee replacement, and physical therapy; high blood pressure and elevated cholesterol counts; stents and bypasses; dialysis and kidney transplants, leukemia and sickle-cell anemia. God cares about diabetes, depression, and dementia; about arthritis, osteoporosis, and paralysis; and about asthma, emphysema, and COPD.

God knows from personal experience in Jesus that when we haven't slept enough, or eaten well, or felt the affirmation of touch, it's harder for us to love well, to think clearly, and to feel truly. Everything that touches our bodies matters to God.

Because God cares about our bodies, God smiles when we relax beside a warm fire on a cold night, when strong and tender hands massage away the knotted tension of stress from our shoulders, and when a welcoming embrace assures us that we belong.

God delights in the three-point shot that ties a game at the buzzer and sends it into overtime, in the perfect spiral pass to the outstretched hands of a sprinting split-end, and in the powerful strokes and swiftly gliding body of a swimmer in the last leg of a 400-meter relay.

A dancer's flowing grace pleases God. So do the breath, hands, and mouths that make music and the eyes and hands that fashion a painting or a sculpture.

God's love for us and for our bodies includes the good gift of sex, which can have nearly sacramental power for celebrating, expressing, deepening, and heightening the intimacy that covenanted lovers share.

God cares about all these things and more because we don't just have bodies, we are bodies. However intellectual, emotional, or spiritual an experience might be, it is also and always a physical experience. It involves our bodies' skeletal, chemical, vascular, muscular, glandular, respiratory, neural, electrical, and digestive systems. All of our experiences fire across the synapses of our brains and register somewhere in our bodies. Indeed, I think our experiences are stored somewhere in our bodies.

Barbara Brown Taylor wrote,

> God loves flesh and blood, no matter what kind of shape it is in. Whether you are sick or well, lovely or irregular, there comes a time when it is vitally important for your spiritual health to drop your clothes, look in the mirror, and say, "Here I am. This is the body-like-no-other that my life has shaped. I live here. This is my soul's address." After you have taken a good look around, you may decide that there is a lot to be thankful for, all things considered. Bodies take real beatings. That they heal from most things is an underrated miracle. That they give birth is beyond reckoning. (*An Altar in the World* [New York: Harper One, 2009] 38)

When you look in the mirror at your body, a gift from God to you, remember that the resurrected Jesus stands beside you, bearing the evidence of his own wounds, now healed. The nail prints are still in his hands. The scar in his side is still visible.

With him at our side, we talk as friends about all the wounding and bruising experiences of our lives. From him, we learn that wholeness does not mean remaining unscarred. Instead, wholeness includes the astonished awareness that our scars are a physical record of God's mercy on us in the hardest seasons of life.

The church, the Apostle Paul never tired of insisting, is "the body of Christ." As God was once in the world in Jesus, so God is now in the world through the wounded but whole people who follow him. We can know how fully and faithfully we represent Jesus by how we treat the bodies of other people.

Catholic priest and controversial activist Daniel Berrigan was exactly right when he said, a bit shockingly, "It all comes down to this: Whose flesh are you touching and why? Whose flesh are you recoiling from and why? Whose flesh are you burning and why?" (quoted by Taylor, 45).

At Christmas, God became flesh and dwelt among us in Jesus. God keeps becoming flesh in you and me. We are Jesus' hands, feet, eyes, ears, and mouth. Jesus is what we say to the world. Jesus is what we do in the world.

We speak as he spoke. We love as he loved. And, amazingly, we see God's glory in one another.

Notes

Notes

BEHOLD
THE LAMB OF GOD
John 1:29-34; 19:28-30

Central Question

What is the purpose of Jesus' life?

Scripture

John 1:29-34

1:29 The next day John saw Jesus coming toward him and said, "Look! The Lamb of God who takes away the sin of the world! 30 This is the one about whom I said, 'He who comes after me is really greater than me because he existed before me.' 31 Even I didn't recognize him, but I came baptizing with water so that he might be made known to Israel." 32 John testified, "I saw the Spirit coming down from heaven like a dove, and it rested on him. 33 Even I didn't recognize him, but the one who sent me to baptize with water said to me, 'The one on whom you see the Spirit coming down and resting is the one who baptizes with the Holy Spirit.' 34 I have seen and testified that this one is God's Son."

John 19:28-30

19:28 After this, knowing that everything was already completed, in order to fulfill the scripture, Jesus said, "I am thirsty." 29 A jar full of sour wine was nearby, so the soldiers soaked a sponge in it, placed it on a hyssop branch, and held it up to his lips. 30 When he had received the sour wine, Jesus said, "It is completed." Bowing his head, he gave up his life.

Reflecting

This has probably been a week of sacrifice in your home. I am not referring to the sacrifice of buying gifts that may have stretched budgets to their limits. Rather, let us consider for just a moment the sacrificial nature of Christmas wrapping paper. I have always had mixed feelings about decorating gifts with such beautiful paper. Why put such glorious wrapping on boxes that are surely going to be torn apart in the excitement of finding out what is inside? As exciting as it is to open presents, to be able to hold a gift in my hands, and to be humbled by the act of love in the giving of the gift, despite all the joy, my heart sinks just a little to see the beautiful paper crumpled and tossed aside.

I suspect that those who were crowded along the banks of the Jordan River listening to the words of John the Baptist as he introduced Jesus to the world would not have had the same issue with wrapping paper as I have. Their upbringing in the traditions of the Jewish faith gave them a deep appreciation for the meaning of sacrifice. The most beautiful wrapping would be used to represent the value of the gift within. Perhaps to those onlookers at the Jordan it would be obvious that it was fitting for John to make a great sacrifice in announcing the importance of one even greater than him.

If John was a great man of God, his greatness was not diminished because his task was to introduce someone even greater. John introduced Jesus to a crowd of people who knew and appreciated the value of sacrifice, so his words of introduction of Jesus must have struck a deep chord with them.

> In what sense was John's willingness to decrease so that Jesus could increase (John 3:30) a "sacrifice"? How is it like or unlike Jesus' own sacrifice? How is it like or unlike the sacrifice God calls me to make?

Studying

"The Lamb of God." John 1:29-34 presents quite a remarkable scene. We can imagine John the Baptist up to his waist in the waters of the Jordan River looking up and seeing in the crowd the Coming One he was telling everyone about. You get the impression as you read this account that the Baptizer was not expecting

to see Jesus at that moment. It's not like they planned ahead of time so that John could formally introduce Jesus to the masses at a designated time and place.

There must have been great excitement in his voice. It makes you wonder how many times he imagined this encounter. How much thought he had previously given to what he might say when, at long last, he and Jesus should meet. Whether his words were spontaneous or planned, John announced the Messiah's presence by calling him "the Lamb of God" (John 1:29). It has become one of history's favorite titles for Jesus.

Though fairly common today, the two encounters with John the Baptist in John 1:29 and 36 are the only places in the Bible where Jesus is called "the Lamb of God." Nor does the title have any clear antecedents in the Old Testament, although it does spring from ancient Jewish traditions and images.

Three possible contexts have been proposed for understanding this powerful image (Culpepper, 496–97). First, there is the *apocalyptic lamb* (or ram), a powerful agent of God found in several Jewish apocalyptic works that overcomes evil and saves God's people (see 1 Enoch 90:38; Rev 5:5-6; 7:17; 17:14). Second is the imagery of the *suffering servant*, an association that derives from the description of this Old Testament figure as "like a lamb being brought to slaughter" (Isa 53:7). This verse is specifically applied to Jesus in Acts 8:32, and the accounts of Jesus' baptism draw on the language of Isaiah 42:1, another passage about Isaiah's "Servant of Yahweh."

Finally, there is the imagery of the *paschal lamb* that was sacrificed at Passover and eaten in remembrance of the lamb's blood sprinkled on the doorposts in the book of Exodus, saving the people of Israel from the angel of death before their flight out of Egypt. Early in the history of the Christian church, the reference to the paschal lamb became the preferred interpretation of the meaning of the phrase "Lamb of God." The Passover story contains elements of protection as well as salvation. Even so, the lamb sacrificed at the Passover is not specifically intended as a sacrifice for sins. In Jewish thinking, its purpose is not to take away the sins of the world (v. 29) but to protect the Israelite slaves from death and, with succeeding observances, to commemorate this turning point in biblical history.

John's declaration seems, therefore, to merge the Passover image with one or both of the others. Like the apocalyptic lamb, the "Lamb of God" deals with human sin. Like the suffering servant, he accomplishes his mission through a path of death and rejection.

The reference to Passover is further strengthened by the prominence of the Passover meal in the Gospels' passion narratives. On the night before his arrest, Jesus connected his coming self-sacrifice to the bread and wine consumed on that sacred occasion. The Fourth Gospel deepens this connection even more by mentioning the detail of the hyssop used to give Jesus a sip of sour wine on the cross (John 19:29). The hyssop branch was used by the Israelites to spread the blood of the lamb above their doors on the first Passover night (Exod 12:22).

John explained what Jesus was to do: he is "the Lamb of God who takes away the sin of the world!" (John 1: 29). It is interesting that such a lowly and defenseless animal would be attached to such grand and powerful work. However, it is a tremendous image of Jesus, whose gentle nature belied his power and the immensity of his mission. That mission was to reshape the relationship between a sinful world and the God who created it. Jesus came to redefine humankind's standing with God.

In John's prologue (vv. 1-18), the writer insists that the Baptizer was only a man sent to direct people's attention to the Word of God. Now we hear him describing his relation to the Messiah in his own voice.

The crowds might have misinterpreted the phrase John used to describe Jesus, "he who comes after me" (John 1:30). This phrase was often used by a teacher in reference to a student or successor who would carry on in the footsteps of the teacher. John did come on the scene before Jesus, and he did draw a significant following. It would have been easy, therefore, for people to misunderstand the relationship between Jesus and John. So John emphasizes the point made in the prologue; that is, that Jesus existed before John and, because of that fact, he should be considered greater than John (v. 30).

John emphasizes that he baptizes with water, but Jesus baptizes with the Holy Spirit. John can testify to this because he witnessed the Holy Spirit coming to Jesus as a dove and resting on him (vv. 31-34). It is the indwelling Holy Spirit within Jesus that opens the eyes of all who see him as the one and only begotten of God, whose mission is to take away the sin of the world. The Baptizer admits twice that he did not recognize Jesus. Rather, the Spirit resting within Jesus opened John's eyes—and can open everyone's eyes—that he is, in fact, the Son of God (v. 34).

"It is completed." No other person has the title and the role of "Lamb of God." Therefore, no other person can take away the sin of the world. No other person can claim the exalted status the Fourth Gospel gives to the Word of God in its prologue. And no other person has such a uniquely intimate connection with God manifested in the Spirit's resting upon him at his baptism. No one else could complete the saving work of God. "It is completed" (John 19:30) is the ultimate victory statement of the only one who could possibly say it.

It may seem odd just a few days after Christmas to focus on a passage that seems better suited for Easter. But John the Baptist helps us see the bigger picture of why Christ came, why "the Word became flesh" (John 1:14).

The meaning of the baby in the manger becomes clear on the cross. The Baptizer's title frames the entire vast, sweeping narrative of God's saving work for humankind. The helpless lamb in the manger is the bearer of God's glory on the cross. That is the "complete" story of Christmas.

Understanding

Christmas is over for another year. A new year will be upon us very soon. This is a good time to put ourselves in John the Baptist's sandals. Like John, we have been through a period of great expectation for the coming of God incarnate. The Baptizer spent considerable time preaching in the desert to prepare people for Jesus' arrival. We, too, have spent a great amount of time preparing for grand celebrations, gift buying, and traveling to commemorate the coming of Christ. Hopefully, the last few weeks also have been a time of spiritual preparation and a time spent in prayer and meditation on the meaning of Christ's coming for you personally and for the world. Now, the big event is over. It is time to take up the meaning of Christmas and move into a new chapter.

For John, the coming of Christ meant it was time for him to fade into the background, but his strong witness and testimony of Jesus never diminished. He carried that message with boldness all the way to his death. Likewise, we must consider how we will carry the message of the Lamb of God into the new year. We must find ways in which an event that happened 2,000 years ago—and which we celebrated last week—can live on through us and into a hopeful future.

Christ's pronouncement on the cross still echoes today, and the salvation story continues. Christ' work is complete, but our work begins anew every day. In our time, when most of the news we see and hear seems bad, it is important to find ways to minister to our darkened world. The Spirit of God that dwelled in Jesus is now the breath of God's church. We have inherited the work of the Baptizer. His words must be ours: behold the Lamb of God!

What About Me

> **What is my response to the completed work of Christ?**

• *Are you a victim of the "post-holiday blues"?* It is a common malady of our time. So much time and energy is spent preparing for the holidays that when they are over, there is sometimes a deep sense of letdown. Yet the message of the season expresses great hope. Are there ways we can allow the meaning of the season to replace the letdown of the big event being over?

• *Is there a new way to think about New Year's resolutions?* This is the week to concentrate on New Year's resolutions. What bad habits will you attempt to let die with the old year? What new habits will you seek to establish in the new year? How can the lessons of John the Baptist introducing the Lamb of God to his followers inform you as you seek to find new and better ways to live out your faith?

• *The humility of the Lamb.* I find it easy to become humble when I remember all the people who have made sacrifices for me. There have been so many people who have given so much that I am ever mindful of how indebted I am for the sacrifices they made on my behalf. There is no way to repay my parents, my wife, or the mentors in my life. However, I can bring my gratitude to the service of others who need my help. The Lamb of God made the ultimate sacrifice. How might our faithful meditation on that key truth change the way in which we see the world?

Resources

R. Alan Culpepper, "Lamb of God," *Mercer Dictionary of the Bible*, ed. Watson E. Mills et al. (Macon GA: Mercer University Press, 1990).

D. Freeman, "Feasts," *The Illustrated Bible Dictionary*, Part 1, ed. J. D. Douglas (Sydney AU: InterVarsity, 1980).

J. C. Rylaarsdam, "Day of Atonement," *The Interpreter's Dictionary of the Bible*, vol. 1 (New York: Abingdon, 1962).

BEHOLD
THE LAMB OF GOD
John 1:29-34; 19:28-30

Introduction

On this last Sunday of the calendar year, we find ourselves in between our celebration of Christmas and our welcoming of the New Year. For many of us, these few days on the threshold of the turning of the calendar will be a time for taking stock of how we invested our time and energy in the year that is ending and clarifying our hopes and dreams for the coming year.

In our sifting of the past year and our planning for the days ahead, it is reassuring and energizing for us to take a close look at what we believe about Jesus and at what difference those beliefs make in how we live. John the Baptist stands ready to help us.

John the Baptist's Testimony

John 1:29-34 is the second section of a larger block of material (John 1:19-34) that provides a compact summary of John's testimony to Jewish leaders from Jerusalem (v. 19). In the first section (vv. 19-28), John responds to questions that certain "priests and Levites" asked him (v. 19), as well as to questions put to him by "those sent by the Pharisees" (v. 24).

The questions the Jerusalem officials posed to John through their emissaries had to do with John's understanding of himself. As he answered their questions, John steadfastly refused to claim any identity for himself other than that of "a voice crying out in the wilderness" (v. 23). He insisted that the greatest significance of his vocation came from his witness to someone greater, whose sandal straps he felt unworthy to untie (vv. 26-27).

In our Advent lessons from the prologue to John's Gospel (1:1-18), we've already explored features of John's witness to Jesus (see John 1:6-8, 15). Today, we give focused attention to verses 29-34, which are essentially John's testimony about Jesus. With the exception of a couple of phrases from the Gospel's narrator in verses 29 and 32, these verses are presented as John's direct description of Jesus. It is a description shaped by John's experience in his baptism of Jesus.

Although the Fourth Gospel doesn't offer a direct account of that baptism, as the other three Gospels do (Mark 1:9-11; Matt 3:13-17; Luke 3:21-22), John the Baptist's testimony in our focal verses echoes that event. His remarkable statements about Jesus remind us of the grace of Jesus, "who takes away the sin of the world" (v. 29), and of the Spirit that "rested" on Jesus (vv. 32-33) and flows through him to us. His grace embraces the year that is ending and his Spirit empowers us for the days ahead.

John declared the identity of Jesus by offering four richly meaningful descriptions of him: Lamb of God (v. 29), the one who preexisted John (v. 30), the one upon whom the Spirit rests (vv. 32-34), and God's Son (v. 34). These descriptions provide a compelling understanding of Jesus' significance. They are in the form of an announcement that John made in response to an appearance of Jesus. This announcement begins with these words: "Look! The Lamb of God who takes away the sin of the world!" (v. 29). There are two other statements revealing Jesus' identity in this same chapter. The next day, when he saw Jesus again, John said to two of his disciples, "Look! The Lamb of God!" (v. 36). The day after that, Nathaniel said to Jesus, "Rabbi, you are God's Son. You are the king of Israel" (v. 49).

Jesus, the Lamb of God

Because verse 35 repeats and reinforces John's declaration that Jesus is the *Lamb of God* (v. 29), we should think of this metaphorical title as his central affirmation of Jesus' identity. It's a title that resonates richly with a cluster of theological themes. Among those themes are: (1) the apocalyptic lamb who triumphs over evil, (2) the suffering and serving lamb who lives and dies on behalf of God's people, and (3) the Passover lamb whose death effects liberation from bondage (Raymond E. Brown, *The Gospel According to John*, vol. 1 [Garden City NY: Doubleday, 1966] 58–63).

There are references in apocalyptic Jewish texts to a *Lamb who vanquishes evil* in the world. For instance, *Testament of Joseph* 19:8 describes a time when "from Judah was born a virgin wearing a linen garment, and from her went forth a Lamb, without spot, and on His left hand there was as it were a lion; and all the beasts rushed against Him, and the lamb overcame them, and destroyed them, and trod them under foot. And because of Him the angels rejoiced, and men, and all the earth. And these things shall take place in their season, in the last days."

The attacking beasts that the Lamb destroyed symbolize the forces of evil that dominated the world until the time of their defeat. Many Christian readers will think of Jesus when they read this text, which likely influenced the vivid imagery the book of Revelation uses to describe the victory of Christ: "They [the allies of evil personified as 'the beast'] will make war on the Lamb, but the Lamb will emerge victorious, for he is Lord of lords and King of kings" (Rev 17:14). In heaven, the saints whom the Lamb delivered "cried out with a loud voice: 'Victory belongs to our God who sits on the throne, and to the Lamb'" (Rev 7:10).

The *idea of a serving and suffering Lamb who lives and dies on behalf of God's people* came from one of the four "Servant Songs" found in the book of Isaiah (42:1-9; 49:1-13; 50:4-11; 52:13–53:12). The language and hopes of those songs shaped how the writers of the New Testament interpreted Jesus' life, death, and resurrection. The last of those songs (Isa 52:13–53:12) acknowledges that the servant "was oppressed and tormented, but didn't open his mouth. Like a lamb brought to slaughter, like a ewe silent before her shearers, he didn't open his mouth" (Isa 53:7; see Acts 8:32). This lamblike servant is the one who carried our "sickness," bore our "sufferings," and was "pierced because of our rebellions and crushed because of our crimes. He bore the punishment that made us whole; by his wounds we are healed" (Isa 52:4-5; see Matt 8:17).

The Gospel of John also draws on the story of the Passover, found largely in Exodus—and especially the image of the *Passover lamb*—in its presentation of the death of Jesus. According to

John, Pilate handed Jesus over to be crucified "about noon on the Preparation Day for the Passover" (John 19:14). That was the time when the priests in the temple began their slaughter of sacrificial lambs.

John 19:29 says that Roman soldiers offered the dying Jesus sour wine in a sponge they had affixed to a hyssop branch. It was with a hyssop branch that Hebrew slaves smeared lamb's blood on the doorposts of their dwellings on the night of their liberation (Exod 12:22).

Finally, Exodus 12:46 tells us that God directed that none of the bones of a Passover lamb should be broken, and John 19:32-35 indicates that, contrary to customary Roman practice, the soldiers did not break Jesus' legs to hasten his death. John's Gospel asserts, "These things happened to fulfill the scripture, *They won't break any of his bones*" (John 19:36).

All three of these themes enrich our understanding of what John the Baptist meant when he announced that Jesus was "the Lamb of God who takes away the sin of the world" (John 1:29). Like the apocalyptic lamb, Jesus has triumphed decisively over the evil forces that oppose life. Like the suffering servant, in lamblike humility, Jesus lived in solidarity with human beings and died on our behalf. Like the Passover lamb, the sacrificial offering of Jesus' life effected our liberation from slavery to oppression and sin.

Jesus, the Preexistent One

John the Baptist also affirmed that Jesus "is the one about whom I said, 'He who came after me is really greater than me because he existed before me'" (John 1:30). It seems likely that John's own disciples felt that because John was older than Jesus and because John's public ministry began before Jesus' ministry did, John had priority over Jesus. John insisted here, as he did in 1:15, that Jesus preexisted him. Therefore, Jesus took precedence over him.

Indeed, as the prologue insists, Jesus preexisted creation itself (1:1-3). John was born into history before Jesus, but Jesus participated in the birth of history itself.

Jesus, the One Upon Whom the Spirit Rests and God's Son

We know from the other three Gospels that when John baptized Jesus, the Spirit descended upon Jesus and a voice from heaven declared him to be God's beloved Son. Referring to his baptism of Jesus, John underscored that the Spirit rested on Jesus (John 1:32-34) and that the abiding of the Spirit confirmed for John that Jesus was God's Son (v. 34).

We've seen the role that the fourth "Servant Song" of Isaiah (Isa 52:13–53:12) played in shaping the Gospel of John's characterization of Jesus as the "Lamb of God." It's likely that the first Servant Song (Isa 42:1-9) helped all the Gospel writers with their understanding and description of Jesus' baptism: "Here is my servant, the one I uphold; my chosen, who brings me delight. I've put my spirit upon him; he will bring justice to the nations" (Isa 42:1). In baptism, God put the Spirit on Jesus. Now, because that Spirit rests on Jesus, he is the conduit of the Spirit for everyone else.

"God's Son" is a title this Gospel often uses for Jesus (see, for example, John 1:14, 18, 34, 49 and 5:1-30). John 3:16-17 affirms God's great love for the Son and, through the Son, for humanity: "God so loved the world that he gave his only Son, so that everyone who believes in him won't perish but will have eternal life. God didn't send his Son into the world to judge the world, but that the world might be saved through him."

Jesus' baptism helped to convince John of Jesus' identity. John knew that because the Spirit rested on Jesus, Jesus was the one who uniquely bore and generously imparted that Spirit to others. When we trust in Jesus, the Spirit descends and remains on us as it did on him. The experience of that Spirit assures us that we are God's beloved children, just as the Spirit confirmed for John that Jesus was God's Son.

The Church Is a Community of Witness

In many ways, the church's role is like that of John the Baptist. God calls us to be a community of witness that points people to Jesus. We tell others what we know about him and what we have experienced with him. Our witness is our own experience of Jesus: we tell what we have seen and heard and felt.

"Witnessing" shouldn't be impersonal and artificial. It isn't memorizing formulas so we can insert them awkwardly into otherwise normal conversations. It isn't turning ordinary encounters into something like sales calls, distorting friends or potential friends into "prospects."

On the contrary, "witnessing" grows from the simple fact that if our experience with Jesus is real and deep, then we cannot help but give evidence of him in our ordinary living, losing, loving, struggling, growing, and celebrating. To witness is simply to tell others what we have been graced to see. C. S. Lewis caught the spirit of this kind of witness when he wrote, "Think of me as a fellow patient in the same hospital who, having been admitted earlier, could give some advice" (quoted by Sheldon Vanauken, *A Severe Mercy* [San Francisco: Harper & Row, 1980] 134).

As the New Year begins, we remember who Jesus is for us and for the world. We allow ourselves to be more deeply immersed in his reality, and we bear witness to what we see, hear, feel, know, and trust.

Notes

Notes

www.ingramcontent.com/pod-product-compliance
Lightning Source LLC
Chambersburg PA
CBHW070551030426
42337CB00016B/2453